Marseille & Montpellier Travel Guide

Attractions, Eating, Drinking, Shopping & Places To Stay

Brendan Kavanagh

Copyright © 2014, Astute Press
All Rights Reserved.

No part of this publication may be reproduced, stored in a retrieval system, or transmitted, in any form or by any means without the prior written permission of the publisher, nor be otherwise circulated in any form of binding or cover other than that in which it is published and without similar condition being imposed on the subsequent purchaser.

If there are any errors or omissions in copyright acknowledgements the publisher will be pleased to insert the appropriate acknowledgement in any subsequent printing of this publication.

Although we have taken all reasonable care in researching this book we make no warranty about the accuracy or completeness of its content and disclaim all liability arising from its use

Table of Contents

Marseille 7
    Culture 8
    Location & Orientation 9
    Climate & When to Visit 10

Sightseeing Highlights 12
    Unité d'Habitation 12
    La Place Castellane 13
    Calanque de Morgiou 14
    Le Cours Julien 15
    Museum of Mediterranean Archaeology 16
    Notre Dame de la Garde 17
    Le Vieux Port (Old Port) 18
    Château d'If 19
    Panier 21
    Parc Balneaire du Prado 22
    Petit Train Marseille 23
    Ferry Boat Ride 25
    Palais & Parc Longchamp 25
    L'Estaque 26

Recommendations for the Budget Traveller 28
    Places to Stay 28
        Hotel La Résidence du Vieux Port Marseille 28
        Best Western La Joliette 29
        Music Hotel 30
        Hotel Lutia 30
        Ibis Gare Saint Charles 31
    Places to Eat & Drink 31
        Four des Navettes 32
        L'Escapade Marseillaise 32
        Le Julien 33
        The Cup of Tea 33
        La Brocéliande 34

- Places to Shop...34
  - Le Centre Commercial les Puces...34
  - The Market at Noailles (Le Marché de Noailles) 35
  - Prado Market 36
  - La Chocolatière du Panier 36
  - Centre Bourse 37

Montpellier 38
- Culture 40
- Location & Orientation...41
- Climate & When To Visit..42

Sightseeing Highlights 44
- Odysseum District...44
  - Planetarium Galilee..45
  - Aquarium Mare Nostrum 46
  - Karting & Bowling 46
  - Ice Skating 47
  - Odysseum Activities 47
- Fabre Museum..48
- Montpellier Zoo 49
- Château Flaugergues...50
- Royal Square of Peyrou 51
- St. Peter's Cathedral 52
- Château de La Mosson 53
- Museum of Anatomy & the Faculty of Medicine.......................54
- Montpellier Historical Centre 55
- Henri Prades Museum..56
- Antigone District 57
- Botanical Gardens...58
- Château de la Mogère...59
- Esplanade Charles de Gaulle 60

Recommendations for the Budget Traveller 61
- Places To Stay...61
  - Montpellier Hostel 61
  - Les Arbousiers...63
  - La Farigoule 64
  - La Vagance 65
  - Sweet Home 34 65
- Places To Eat & Drink 66
  - Playfood 66
  - Le P'tit Mas..67

Le Pescator..67
Pain et Cie...68
Times Café..69
Places To Shop **69**
Les Halles Castellane 69
Peyrou Plaza...70
Images du Demain 71
Le Boutik'R...72
Etat d'Ame..73

Marseille

Often hidden in the shadows of Paris, Marseille is the second most populous city in France with the largest port in the Mediterranean. Sitting upon the French Riviera, Marseille embraces a diverse culture of individuals. Its location across from North Africa is reflected in its ambience, specifically noticeable when visiting sites like the colorful Noailles market.

If you were to compare Marseille to the larger Paris, you would find that it is quite different indeed. Without the language similarities, you may even think you are in another country altogether. Its cliffs and fjords (clanques), sea views, beaches and harbors define the scenery of the city. In fact, its port welcomes over 2 million people per year. This is something that landlocked Paris lacks.

Cruise ships bring passengers to the city as well so that they can enjoy not only the beach scene, but also its history, museums, theaters, and architecture.

Culture

Marseille is actually one of the oldest cities in Europe, founded in 600 B.C. by the Phoceans. Its population of 1 million is a melting pot of culture. Besides its French citizens, a number of Spanish and Italians who immigrated to the city after World War II have also left their mark on the city. This diversity is also apparent when visiting its incredible restaurants and cafes.

It is this diverse culture that the city celebrates regularly with its many festivals throughout the year. One of the most popular is the Avec le Temps, taking place in springtime at Espace Julien: one of Marseille's concert halls. Avec le Temps showcases and celebrates native French artists who represent all different types of music. Moving toward the end of June, La Fête Bleue (The Blue Festival) is celebrated annually. This is a festival during which entertainment in all forms is offered with the theme being the color blue, as the name states.

Also in June, toward the end of the month, is La Fête du Panier; as it offers shows, concerts and different shopping experiences in the oldest part of the city. Another popular festival in Marseille that lasts all summer is Le FDAmM or Festival de Danse et des Arts Multiples de Marseille. Le FDAmM is an art festival, primarily dance, which exists as a way for artists to gain exposure within the city.

Heading into September is the ten-year-old music festival known as Marsatac. There is also a World Music festival known as La Fiesta Des Duds, held at Dock des Suds in October. Besides music, Marseille also celebrates the holidays, as exhibited during La Foire aux Santons. This is a popular Christmas market that is held near Vieux Port from late November through December.

Location & Orientation

Marseille is located on the Mediterranean Sea in the middle of the French Riviera. A wide boulevard called, the Canebière, cuts through the city as it starts at Vieux Port (the Old Port) and stretches east toward the Réformés quarter. In the Bay of Marseille, are four islands that compose the Frioul Archipelago.

About 30 km from the city is its airport, Marseille-Provence International Airport. From the airport, visitors can access Marseille by bus, taxi, or train. The main train station is St. Charles, which is within walking distance to the Old Port and Canebière. The train station is accessible by bus or by two subway lines. The bus station is right next to the train station.

Getting to Marseille from other French cities is quite easy. However, once arriving in the city, do not be intimidated or discouraged by its public transportation. It is actually encouraged to use, since driving in the center of the city can be torturous. If you are driving into the city center, be sure to park it in a reputable location and switch to public transportation. Subways operate until 10:30 p.m. except on weekends when they close at 12:30 a.m.

Trams run until 12:30 a.m. seven days per week. Busses, however, stop operating around 9:00 p.m. usually. If you are on a bus route and need to get somewhere after 9:00 p.m., be ready to take a taxi.

One way to get to Marseille is by ferry boat, which is an attraction by itself. It crosses the Vieux Port (the Old Port) and is known as the shortest boat ride in Europe.
Since Marseille is a large city, visitors should be aware that there are certain areas to avoid, as is the case in most large cities. Smart tourists wear money belts and avoid carrying anything of too much value.

It is advisable to avoid many of the northern neighborhoods at night, as well as Gare St. Charles. Also, if driving a car, be sure to keep the doors locked. The city center is quite congested and people on motorbikes have been known to open car doors with the driver inside, while quickly snatching purses and valuables and then speeding away. This does not mean that you should be paranoid, however. Marseille is generally a safe city. Just be smart and aware of your surroundings.

Climate & When to Visit

Marseille's climate is a typical Mediterranean one with warm, dry summers and humid, mild winters. Its coldest months are December through February when the temperatures are an average 54 °F (12 °C). Its warmest months, like in most cities in Europe, are July and August when temperatures average 86 °F (30 °C).

During the winter and spring, Marseille experiences the Mistral, a cold and bitter wind that originates in the Rhône valley. Its proximity to the Sahara Desert also means that it can experience a Sirocco, a warm wind that carries sand from Africa, across the Mediterranean.

Summertime is obviously the most popular time to visit Marseille, since this is when most people take their vacations. However, its warm climate is generally nice all year round.

If you want to experience the warmer weather while avoiding the crowds, plan your visit during late spring or early autumn. Definitely avoid Marseille in July if you do not like crowds. This is when the entire country celebrates Bastille Day. In Marseille, the festivities last approximately two weeks and are quite exciting with plenty of entertainment to keep revelers happy.

Sightseeing Highlights

Unité d'Habitation

280 Bd Michelet
13008 Marseille France
+33 491 16 7800
http://www.marseille-citeradieuse.org/

As a product of modern urban architect, Le Corbusier, Unité d'Habitation is also known as "the house of the foolish" (la maison du fada). By others more optimistic, it is referred to as, "the radiant city."

The building represents the architect's dedication to improving living conditions for residents of crowded cities. His point of view was that people need to feel like part of a community in order to be a successful and productive social unit. Without a close-knit community, people feel too scattered to have a connection. And furthermore, without this connection, people fail to respect each other.

So by offering housing units, such as the Unité d'Habitation, Le Corbusier was able to test this theory. Although people who reside in his housing units live in separate dwellings; the building has a communal shopping area, church, and school for children of the community. There is also a bar and restaurant on the third floor. Between 10 a.m. and 6 p.m., visitors can access the roof where there is a stunning view of the sea and hills that surround Marseille.

The huge roof terrace of the building has magnificent panoramic views. Recently, it was taken over by designer, Ito Morabito; who also goes by the name, Ora Ïto. He bought the 6,500 square foot (600 meter) in 2010. Originally designed to be a gymnasium, it has recently been restored with plans for a bookshop, café, and exhibition space.

La Place Castellane

Intersection of Boulevard Baille,
Avenue du Prado and Rue de Rome

La Place Castellane is actually a roundabout at the intersection of Boulevard Baille, Rue de Rome, and Avenue du Prado. In the middle, there is a fountain and sculpture, difficult to miss with its tall column erupting from the center.

La Place Castellane is not so much an attraction but a location that serves as a meeting point before heading to one of the many cafes and cinemas that surround it. It is named after Marquis de Castellane-Majastre who donated the land and financed the project.

There are two metro lines, numbers one and two, which service La Place Castellane. Be sure not to confuse La Place Castellane with La Castellane. The latter is one of the poor suburbs of Marseille.

Calanque de Morgiou

The Calanques are a collective group of small fjords that are located south of Marseille, near Cassis. The view is stunning with a clear blue sea set below limestone cliffs. Whether you view the Calanques from the sea or from the cliffs, you are sure to get incredible views. Just keep in mind that the hike up the cliffs can be quite arduous. The trail leading up to the Calanques (GR) is marked with white and red stripes and is easy to find.

Although all of the fjords offer a great view, the Calanque de Morgiou is the largest of them. It was formerly a fishing port when tuna fishing was popular during the 17th century. The fishing cabins still exist today but they are used for tourism purposes instead of for fishing.

Another reason for the popularity of the Calanque de Morgiou is the Cosquer cave. This is an underwater grotto with multiple cave drawings that date back over 27,000 years.

To reach Calanque de Morgiou, you can either take a boat or a bus. Different tour companies offer boat access. If taking the bus, take the #21 bus to the University campus at Luminy. The busses to Luminy leave from Vieux Port and Rond Point du Prado. The ride to Luminy takes only about 20 minutes. Once there, a 15 minute walk takes you to a location where you have the choice to head up to a lookout point or down to the Clanque. If you head up, the walk is approximately 20 minutes along a ridge. The descent takes about a half hour.

These are the two most popular options and you can see people coming and going throughout the day when the weather is warm. There are other options for those more adventurous as well. Be sure to bring water for your hike as well as your bathing suit should you care to swim in the beautiful water below. Also, be aware that some of the Calanques may be closed from the months of June to September when there can be a high fire risk.

Le Cours Julien

http://coursjulien.marsnet.org/

The Cours Julien is a partially pedestrianized road in the 6th arrondissement. The neighborhood is composed of artists, musicians, and free spirits. Before 1970, farmers would congregate in the main courtyard to sell their produce. Now it serves as a beautiful garden that transforms into a pedestrian zone with attractive fountains and garden greenery. It is a trendy area with theaters, concert halls, bars and restaurants abundant.

What makes Le Cours Julien interesting is that it is situated right in the middle of the hustle and bustle of the city. Its car-free zones, laid back mood, and general quaintness seem to be protesting against the big city vibe. It is easily accessible, only a 15 minute walk from the Vieux Port. If making a visit to the area, try to avoid Sundays and Mondays when restaurants and shops tend to be closed.

Museum of Mediterranean Archaeology

Centre de la Vieille Charité, 2 Rue de la Charité
+33 491 14 5880
http://www.muselia.com/france/marseille/museum-of-mediterranean-archaeology/2979

The Museum of Mediterranean Archaeology is one of the oldest museums in Marseille. From its establishment in 1863 until 1989, its home was Château Borély before moving to the Vieille Charité building.

Although the museum houses other tenants, the museum occupies most of the first floor. It is within these walls where you can find an overview of the ancient civilizations that once occupied the banks of the Mediterranean Sea, including one of the largest collections of Egyptological artifacts in France.

There is a separate area dedicated to Cyprus, Etruria, Rome, and Greece. Another area is devoted to Mediterranean prehistory from 1 A.D. until the 7th century. With Marseille's long history under Greek rule, visitors are allowed to see a glimpse of the everyday life of the Greek people who lived in the region centuries ago.

To get to the museum by metro, get off at the Joliette stop. The museum is open daily from 10 a.m. until 5 p.m.

Notre Dame de la Garde

Rue Fort du Sanctuaire, 13006
+33 491 13 4080
http://www.notredamedelagarde.com/

Notre Dame de la Garde (meaning Our Lady of the Guard) is a famous Catholic Basilica in Marseille. This Neo-Byzantine-style church was built by architect, Henri-Jacques Espérandieu and touches the sky above Marseille as it sits 490 feet (149 meters) high on a hill south of Vieux Port.

Every year on Assumption day, August 15th, people make the pilgrimage to this church that dates back to the 13th century. Residents of Marseille consider Notre-Dame de la Garde as a protector and guardian of the city. It is also sometimes called "the good mother" (la bonne mère).

Although the Basilica dates back to the year 1214, the current building is actually a replacement of the original. There is a lower church (or crypt) carved from rock, Romanesque style, as well as a Neo-Byzantine style upper church which is decorated by mosaics. From outside the church, you'll notice a 135 foot (41 meter) square bell tower, a 42 foot (12.5 meter) belfry, and a 27 foot (11.2 meter) statue of the Madonna and Child made of copper and gold leaf.

During the years between 2001 and 2008, the Basilica went through an extensive restoration. This was due to the effects of candle smoke on the mosaics, as well as bullets from World War II during the liberation of France. It has also been discovered that the limestone that was used to build the Basilica is sensitive to atmospheric corrosion.

From March to September, the Basilica observes summer hours and offers mass on Sundays at 8 a.m., 9 a.m., 10 a.m., 11 a.m., noon, and 5 p.m. The 9 a.m. and 11 a.m. masses are in the crypt. On weekdays, mass takes place in the crypt at 7:25 a.m., 9 a.m., and 5 p.m. in the crypt. On Saturdays, it takes place at 5 p.m. in the Basilica.

From October 1st through April 1st, the Basilica observes winter hours and offers mass on Sundays at 8 a.m., 9 a.m., 10 a.m., 11 a.m., noon, and 4:30 p.m. The 9 a.m. and 11 a.m. masses are in the crypt. On weekdays, mass takes place in the crypt at 7:25 a.m., 9 a.m., and 4:30 p.m. in the crypt. On Saturdays, it takes place at 4:30 p.m. in the Basilica.

Le Vieux Port (Old Port)

Le Vieux Port (or Old Port) is located at the end of the Canebière, the historic main street that runs through the old quarter of Marseille. It is the natural harbor of the city as well as the center of the city, even if not geographically. This is where everything happens.

The history of the Old Port dates back to 600 BC when Greeks from Phocaea landed there by ship. They set up a trading post and it is still used as a marketplace today as people enjoy watching the fishermen auction off their catches of the day. During the Middle Ages, cannabis was grown in order to produce rope for the mariners and fishermen. This is where the name, Canebière, originated.

Unfortunately, much of the Old Port is not so old after all. Since it was left in ruins during World War II's Battle of Marseille, much of it had to be reconstructed. Today, the Old Port still serves as a marina, a stop for cruise ships and local boat trips, as well as a thriving fish market.

A huge rejuvenation project recently revamped the Port since it was designated as the 2013 European Capital of Culture. It is for this reason that the Old Port may be a bit more popular now amongst tourists than ever before. When visiting the port, it may be best to avoid having an itinerary. Since it is closed off to vehicles, it is a great place to simply walk around and absorb the sights, sounds, and flavors that the area has to offer.

Château d'If

Embarcadère Frioul If,
1 Quai de la Fraternité
+33 496 11 0350
http://www.if.monuments-nationaux.fr/

Located on the island of If, the smallest of the islands in the Frioul Archipelago, is the Château d'If. Despite being referred to as a château, it has been used as both a fortress and a prison. It was made famous by the popular novel by Alexandre Dumas, *The Count of Monte Cristo*.

The island itself spans 11 square miles (30 square kilometers) and is uninhabited apart from the château. Slightly intimidating, the château is a three story building, square shaped, with walls that are 90 feet long (28 meters) on each side. Three gun towers stand guard the way they did in 1524 when King Francis I chose the island for its strategic location for protection from sea attacks.

Château d'If may have been a better prison than a fortress. Its dangerous currents and remote location made it virtually escape-proof and one of the most feared prisons in France. Despite the characters escaping from the prison in the book, The Count of Monte Cristo; no one has ever really escaped. Still, visitors to the prison can find cells named after the two characters: Edmond Dantès and Abbé Faria.

The château was used as a prison until the end of the 19th century and was opened to the public in 1890. It is now a popular tourist destination and can be reached by boat from the Old Port.

From May 16th through September 16th, Château d'If is open daily from 9:30 am until 6:10 p.m.

From September 17th through March 31st, it is open every day but Mondays from 9:30 a.m. until 4:45 p.m. From April 1st through May 15th, it is open daily from 9:30 a.m. until 4:45 p.m.

Adult admission is 5,50 €. Children under 18 free.

Boats leave from the Old Port. Schedules are available on the Frioul If Express website.

Panier

(Neighborhood to the north of the Old Port)

Just north of the Old Port is a neighborhood with tall and narrow houses sat amongst steep steps and wash lines: Panier. This is the oldest part of Marseille and is steeped in history. This is where the Greeks first settled when they arrived in the city in 600 BC.

Since then, a variety of immigrants followed. The area's name comes from a 17th century inn called, Le Logis du Panier. Panier means "basket" in French.

Unfortunately, just like the Old Port, Panier was not immune to the effects of World War II. Although some antiquity has survived, post-war architecture is visible, mainly in the form of granite apartment blocks that divide Panier from the Old Port. Still, it maintains its vibrant diversity that was established by immigrants centuries ago.

Depending on your personality, you may want to either avoid or flock to Panier during the midde to end of June. This is when France's biggest street party occurs: Fête du Panier, taking place on or near midsummer's night.

Community events and children's shows commence the festivities during the afternoon hours. The party heads into the evening with plenty of live, world music and a unique atmosphere. You can wander the street stalls, sampling a culinary tour of the different ethnicities that exist within the community.

Many parts of the Panier are pedestrian-only after 11:30 a.m. with the exception of the Petit Train. An attraction in itself, it makes one Panier stop: at the Vieille Charité. This is an old monument in the middle of the neighborhood that hosts different exhibitions from time to time.

There is also an informative self-guided walking tour to be followed by the plaques set in the ground at various locations. There is no need to follow a strict itinerary, however. Simply allow yourself a couple hours to stroll around, possibly stopping in a gallery or shopping for local crafts.

To get to the Panier, simply walk north from the Old Port. Or catch the Petit Train, for a guided tour.

Parc Balneaire du Prado

Promenade Georges Pompidou
+33 491 55 2551

Created from the land excavated after making Marseille's metro in 1970, is man-made beach area, Parc Balnéaire du Prado. The 1 km long beach is actually five separate beaches that start at the city center and span five kilometers south. The names of the beaches from north to south are Plage du Prado Nord, Plage du Prado Sud, Plage Borély, Plage Bonneveine, and Plage Vieille Chapelle.

Although the quality of the water is dependent upon other factors and sometimes not of the best swimming quality, the beaches themselves are quite nice. They have showers, public toilets, first aid stations, lifeguards, and free lockers for those who want to keep their valuables safe while enjoying the beach scene. There is a children's playground at Borély and Prado du Nord. Borély and Bonneveine both have lounge chairs and umbrellas available to rent.

The popluar Fête du Vent takes place at these beaches every September. This is a festival that pays homage to the otherwise cursed Mistral wind (a hot wind that blows north from Africa). It is celebrated with hundreds of colored kites flying over the Mediterranean. On an annual basis, more than 100,000 people visit the festival.

One common way to get to Parc Balneaire du Prado is to take bus #83 which you can catch at the Old Port and take straight to the start of the park.

Petit Train Marseille

176 Quai du Port

+33 491 25 2469
http://www.petit-train-marseille.com/

Marseille's Petit Train (little train) is a fun way to see the city. You will recognize it when you see it, with its distinct white and blue colors, resembling a toy train of sorts. The train has a few routes from which to choose.

Route 1 goes to Notre Dame de la Garde. It starts at the Old Port and leads through the Corniche seafront and then up to the basilica where you can observe stunning views of the city from above. During high season (April through November), the train departs every 20 minutes, daily. During low season (December through March), the train runs every half hour, daily. The cost during high season is 8 €. During low season, it is 7 €. Children ages 3 – 11 are always 4 €.

Another route called "Le Vieux Marseille" (The Old Marseille), takes you to the old parts of the city with a few different hotel and museum stops. This is the route that takes visitors to the Panier. This route operates daily from April 1st through November 15th, with trains leaving every 30 minutes. The cost during the month of April is 6 €. After May 1st, it is 7 €. Children ages 3 – 11 are always 3 €.

The third route is the Friuli route which leaves from Port Friuli on Ratonneau Island. It operates during high season from June 15th through September 1st, with trains leaving every 30 minute. The cost is 4 € for adults and 2 € for children ages 3 – 11.

Ferry Boat Ride

Marseille's ferry boats are not only a mode of transportation but an attraction as well. The service, which crosses the Old Port every few minutes, is entirely free of cost. You can catch the ferry between the Rive Neuve and the Town Hall (La Mairie). Although it is fairly new, commencing in 2010, it has seen its share of technical problems. For this reason, it is frequently out of service. However, there are other options for crossing the port, which include the historic ferry boat, César.

There is also an option that is not free, but not too expensive either, at 3 € for a 40 minute trip. It is a new fast boat called the batobus, or navette. They run once per hour and leave from the same stop as the Château d'If at the Old Port.

Palais & Parc Longchamp

Boulevard du Jardin Zoologique

Despite its name, Palais Longchamp is not a palace at all. It is a monument created in celebration of the construction of the Marseille canal which brought water from the Durance River to an otherwise dry Marseille.

One wouldn't think such a city on the sea would have water shortages, but it only receives an average of two rainy days per month during the high part of summer. It is for this reason that a monument was devoted to a much appreciated canal at a volatile time in the 19th century.

Not only did the canal supply a water source, but it also connected the city to the rest of the national waterways. This opened up important trading routes.

The canal is 50 miles (80 km) long with over 10 of those miles underground. It took 15 years to complete before being opened in 1849. It was used as a primary water source since 1970. Now it stands as a glorious monument to the appreciation for the element of water with its fountains, columns, staircases and arches.

The Parc Longchamp surrounds the monument which sits in a suburb east of Saint Charles Station. The park is a beautiful sight alone as well.

L'Estaque

Just west of Marseille is a town known as L'Estaque. In French (Provençal), L'Estaque means "the mooring that attaches boats to the wharf." It became a manufacturing town during the late 1800s when the population exploded.

But what made it even more popular was the way it was seen through the eyes of the artists who appreciated it. Renoir, Cézanne, Braque, and more have all painted popular works of art inspired by L'Estaque. There is even a self-guided walking tour marked by various plaques around the town that can help visitors see through the eyes of the artists themselves.

Paul Cézanne may be the most famous artist to have glorified L'Estaque with the use of a paint brush. He first discovered the area in 1864 but came and went multiple times after that, including the time he returned in order to avoid being drafted to fight in the Franco-Prussian War.

There was one house that he always stayed at next to the church at Place Malterre. This location is now marked with a plaque and is visible as part of the self-guided walking tour. The image of L'Estaque that Cézanne tried to portray was that of a deep blue sea with plenty of red roofs looking down at it, always with plenty of light from the sun.

If you are in the area late in the summer, be sure to visit L'Estaque's annual festival, which takes place the first weekend in September. People come from all over to see their water jousting tournament.

L'Estaque can be easily reached by bus, metro, and train. From Marseille's Saint Charles Station, take the Blue Coast Train which makes regular stops. Or take the metro's line 2 toward Bougainville or tram line 2 to Joliette, then bus 35 to L'Estaque. Although it is easily accessible and now part of Marseille's 16th arrondissement, it has a completely distinguishable identity and atmosphere, making it well worth a visit.

Recommendations for the Budget Traveller

Places to Stay

Hotel La Résidence du Vieux Port Marseille

18, Quai du Port
+33 491 91 9122
http://www.hotel-residence-marseille.com/

The Hotel La Résidence du Vieux Port Marseille was completely renovated in 2010 in the style of post-war modernism with tributes to Le Corbusier and Charlotte Perriand. It offers great sea views from most of its rooms as well as views of Basilica Notre Dame. Its lowest cost rooms offer a view of a quiet pedestrian street and cost 100 € per night. Breakfast is optional at an additional 18€ per night.

Best Western La Joliette

49 Avenue Robert Schuman
+33 145 74 7672
http://www.hotel-joliette.com/

The Best Western La Joliette is a cozy, clean hotel located in a quiet neighborhood accessible by the Joliette metro station. It is situated in a convenient location near the Old Port and the Panier. Rooms have the vibe of a ship's cabin, but are designed elegantly in a way to pay homage to the rich shipping trade of the area. A typical room costs 189 €.

Music Hotel

12 Bld Salvator, 13006 Marseille, France
+33 491 02 1021
http://www.music-hotel.net/

The Music Hotel is a unique hotel with a contemporary theme and courteous staff. It is in a prime location within a 10 minute walk to the Vieux Port. Music Hotel offers free WiFi, large bathrooms with tubs, and optional breakfast for 10 € extra per person. Rooms start at 79 €.

Hotel Lutia

31 Avenue du Prado
+33 491 17 7140
http://www.hotelutia.com/

The Hotel Lutia offers basic accommodations in a great location near the Old Port. Rates start as low as 47 € per night and include free WiFi. The owner is friendly and courteous.

Ibis Gare Saint Charles

Square Narvick
Esplanade Saint Charles
(+33) 491 95 6209
http://www.ibis.com/

The Ibis Marseille Gare Saint Charles is a 172 room hotel with modern and convenient rooms that start at a rate of 71€ per night with free WiFi. The hotel is within walking distance to the train station, Saint Charles. There is also a good restaurant on site.

Places to Eat & Drink

Although the Old Port is obviously the most populous in terms of dining choices, there are too many good restaurants to count in Marseille. Cours Julien is also a popular place to wander around until you find the right choice for your mood, as it is a pedestrian-only street with plenty of affordable restaurants and bars.

Four des Navettes

136 Rue Sainte,
+33 491 33 3212
http://www.fourdesnavettes.com/fr/

Four des Navettes is a famous Marseille bakery located next to the St. Victor Fort. As the name states, it is famous for its navettes, which are a culinary specialty in the city. These dry, boat shaped biscuits are flavored with orange flower and orange zest. The bakery has been open since 1781 and the recipe has been kept secret for about a century.

Four des Navettes is open from 7 a.m. until 8 p.m. daily except for Sundays when it opens from 9 a.m. until 1 p.m. and again from 3 – 7:30 p.m.

L'Escapade Marseillaise

48 Rue Caisserie, behind the Hôtel de Ville
+33 491 31 6169

L'Escapade Marseillaise is a favorite local hangout with typical Provençale cuisine and reasonable prices. It is open for lunch Mondays through Wednesdays from 11:30 – 2:30. On Thursdays through Saturdays, it reopens for dinner from 7:30 – 11:30. It is closed on Sundays.

Le Julien

114 Rue Paradis
+33 491 37 0622
http://www.lejulien.com/

Le Julien is a traditional French restaurant with reasonable prices as well as great food and ambiance. They also sell some of their products such as foie gras, chocolate, and wine baskets to take home as gifts. The restaurant is open for lunch Mondays through Fridays noon until 2: p.m., and dinner Tuesday through Saturday 7:30 p.m. until 10:30 p.m. Reservations are accepted.

The Cup of Tea

1 Rue Caisserie
+33 491 90 8402

This charming café is not only a place to stop for a spot of tea, but also a charming literary café. Indoors, you will find 50 varieties of tea as well as a library and exhibition space. Outside sits a gorgeous terrace on which to sit and sip. The Cup of Tea is open from 8:30 a.m. until 7:00 p.m. Mondays through Fridays. On Saturdays, they open an hour later at 9:30 a.m. The restaurant is closed on Sundays.

La Brocéliande

9 rue Euthymènes
+33 491 54 3378
http://www.taverne-broceliande.com/

When in France, it would be a sin to avoid sampling a variety of crepes, the delicately thin pancake of the country. La Brocéliande is a traditional creperie and restaurant in the Old Port, offering a variety of French dishes at reasonable prices.

It is open Tuesdays through Fridays for lunch, from noon until 2:30 p.m. Dinner is served Tuesday through Thursday between 7:30 and 10:30 and on Fridays from 7 p.m. until midnight. On Saturdays, it is open from noon until midnight. And on Sundays, from noon until 10:30 p.m.

Places to Shop

Le Centre Commercial les Puces

130 Chemin de la Madrague de la Ville
+33 491 58 5252
http://www.centrecommerciallespuces.com/

Le Centre Commercial les Puces is a large flea market in Marseille where you can find everything from fruit to antiques. With over 300 stalls, you are sure to find some unique items. It is open every day except Mondays from 8:30 a.m. until 7:30 p.m.

The Market at Noailles (Le Marché de Noailles)

Canebiere and Capucins

If you go to any of the local markets that occupy Marseille, be sure to stop at the Market at Noailles, also known as the Marché des Capucins. It is located amongst the narrow streets that surround the top of the Canebière, just a short walk from the Old Port. This is the area around the Noailles subway station, which is one of the most interesting, diverse and colorful areas of the city.

The neighborhood hosts an Arabic and Indo-Chinese population which is reflected in the goods that are sold here. A walk through the market here could easily convince you that you are at a bazaar in Algeria. Although it is a bit crowded and chaotic, it is certainly colorful and great for both shopping and people watching.

Spices, rugs, African and Asian goods, as well as more traditional Provençal items can all be found here. It is open from 8 a.m. until 7 p.m. Mondays through Saturdays.

Prado Market

Avenue du Prado

The Prado Market is located along Avenue du Prado between the Castellane metro station and the Périer metro station. Here you can find a wide variety of clothing articles, specialty items, fruits and vegetables. On Friday mornings, there is also a flower market. The Prado Market is open daily between 8 a.m. and 1 p.m.

La Chocolatière du Panier

47 Rue du Petit Puits
+33 491 91 7970
http://lachocolatieredupanier.skyrock.com/

Satisfy your sweet tooth with some amazing and unique chocolate flavors at family-owned La Chocolatière du Panier. Here you can find a variety of unique chocolate treats in 300 different flavors that include onion and lavender, varying depending on what is in season at the time.

The chocolate shop is open on Mondays through Saturdays from 10 a.m. until 1 p.m. and then it reopens from 2:30 p.m. until 6:30 p.m.

Centre Bourse

17 Cours Belsunce
+33 491 14 0050
http://www.centre-bourse.com/30-8284-Accueil.php

Marseille's Bourse Shopping Center is the city's answer to a traditional shopping mall. With all of the street markets that dot the city, it really seems like a shame to spend your shopping experience indoors at a mall, but Centre Bourse offers a family-friendly shopping and entertainment experience if you want to avoid the hustle and bustle of the traditional street markets.

Centre Bourse is less than a five-minute walk from the Old Port and offers approximately 60 different shops and restaurants It is located in the safe area of Jardin des Vestiges, with three floors and a large mezzanine. If you are looking for brand names, this is probably the only place in Marseille where you will find them.

The Centre Bourse is very easy to find. If you are walking, simply head down the Canebiére, toward the Old Port. The entrance to the mall is on the right, across from Ironwood St.

The mall is open Mondays through Saturdays from 9:30 a.m. until 7:30 p.m.

Montpellier

The city of Montpellier covers 60km² and is built on two hills, with the highest point being Place de Peyrou at 57 metres. The two hills, Montpellier and Montpelliéret, give the narrow city streets differences in altitude which in turn gives a cosy feel to this ancient town.

The River Letz winds through the city on its way to the Mediterranean Sea some 16 kilometres distant and the port of Lattes. Montpellier found fortune in the 13th century when Jewish and Arab traders arrived bringing with them silk, spices and sugar. The same trading partners taught the students and merchants of Montpellier a great deal about the world as well as Arabic medicine.

In 1181 Lord Guilhem VIII declared that medicine could be taught by anyone in the city and so the Medical College was born. In the occidental world it is still the oldest operating medical school in the world.

This once sleepy and quiet French city has changed more in the last four decades that it did in the previous three centuries. In the 1960's when 15,000 Algerians fled to France to escape persecution in their own country they descended on Montpellier.

The idyllic existence of the residents was suddenly awakened by the vibrant energy of individuals who were used to the noise and colour of Arab markets. They set about injecting their own lifestyle into the laid-back French way of life and work and helped bring prosperity to the city.

The city is lighthearted and friendly and is fast overtaking Marseille and Nîmes as the best place to live or visit on the coast of southern France. It attracts students in their thousands and it can sometimes be hard to find anyone that was actually born locally. Montpellier has an excellent reputation for being a high-tech town and attracts many computer and technology experts. In the mid 1960's IBM opened their largest European site there.

Culture

The capital of the Languedoc Roussillon area is arguably the most elegant spot on the south coast and certainly pulls in the holidaymakers, nearly 20,000 visitors come to Montpellier every year. This super French city offers more than wonderful architecture, shady traffic-free plazas and boulevards. There is a history and culture with the added bonus of the beach and sparkling Mediterranean Sea only a short drive away.

Modern, chic wine bars, electronic music, designer boutiques and galleries abound to cater for the younger set but there are still more than enough bars, shops and restaurants for the rest of the residents and tourists alike. Take a walk through the city by starting at Place du Comédie then go up rue de la Loge into L'Ecusson where halfway along is the Place Jean-Jaurés. A little further on is Place Marché Aux Fleurs and these are two of the best and busiest places for some people-watching over an aperitif as the sun goes down.

The city is busy and has an energetic feel to it, helped along by the 20% of the population who are students. The academic year is busy but in some ways the best to time to visit as festivals and exhibitions bring colour and excitement to the city.

Mid-June to Mid-July hosts the Le Printemps des Comédiens which is a live entertainment based festival with up to 25 shows of music, culture and circus events. June and July are busy months as the Montpellier Dance festival is in June and the Le Festival de Radio-France et de Montpellier is a music festival in late July. For film buffs the Festival du Cinéma Méditerranéen is in the second half of October and the beginning of November.

Location & Orientation

The city of Montpellier in a few kilometres inland from the Mediterranean Sea on the south coast of France and is halfway between the Spanish and Italian borders, 700 kilometres south east of Paris. There has always been a significant Spanish population and the influence of this can be seen all over the city.

The capital of the Languedoc Roussillon region has seven official districts; divided into sub-districts each with its own council. Ranking 15th in the biggest metropolitan list in France the city population in 2009 was 255,080 with 550,000 in the whole area. It is the fastest growing city in France and the third largest on the Mediterranean coast after Nice and Marseille. In the city itself 43% of the population is under the age of 30.

For getting to Montpellier from other countries there is an airport four kilometres from the city centre. Flights to London are available all year round with seasonal flights from other UK destinations. The Montpellier – Méditerranée Airport offers flights to major airports within Europe as well as to Madeira and North Africa.

The public transport in the city is managed by Transports de l'agglomération de Montpellier (TaM), who look after the parking facilities in the city and the four lines of the tramway. The trams are brightly painted and easy to spot as they glide through the streets. The main railway station is Gare St. Roch which is a stone's throw from the Place Du Comédie and the heart of the city. High speed TGV trains depart from Montpellier to all of the main stations in France.

The tourist office sells the Montpellier CITY card for €20, this allows free use of public transport and free entry into some of the main attractions.

Getting around Montpellier is easy and if your hotel is close to the station why not take a walk in the sunshine. Alternatively there are buses and taxis or why not hire a bicycle. The Vélomagg bike sharing scheme started in 2007 and there are 50 bike stations and 1200 bicycles.

Climate & When To Visit

Montpellier has a Mediterranean climate that is mild with dry, hot summers and moderate winters but there can be wide seasonal differences.

Spring is lovely and the weather can be pleasant with warm sunny days. This time of year is ideal for sightseeing as it is not too hot and there are fewer crowds. Daytime temperatures reach a high of 21°C with a low of 5°C. In summer the weather can get really hot but the ocean breeze from the Mediterranean Sea helps make the climate more comfortable. For beach lovers a high of 29ªC is great for a lazy day sunbathing. A low of 14° is pleasant for taking a stroll round in the evening and sitting down with a chilled glass of wine, French of course.

Autumn can be great but the temperature drops quickly midway through the season. The high of 15°C at the start of the season very quickly dives down to a low of 5°C as winter approaches. The Christmas season brings with it a high of just 12°C and a chilly low of 1°C. For ski lovers there are many resorts within approximately three hours drive of Montpellier.

Sightseeing Highlights

Odysseum District

www.aquariummarenostrum.fr
www.planetarium-galilee.montpellier-agglo.com/
www.centre-commercial-odysseum.com/

There is so much to do at the Odysseum that there might not be time to sit down but if you need to rest you weary feet find the large open arena-style area.

This central point is a good meeting place or you can just sit and relax in the company of statues of historical figures. De Gaulle, Churchill, Mao, Ghandi, Mandela and Golda Meir are just a few of the famous names round the arena. With the brightly painted buildings and palm trees rustling in the breeze the Odysseum has a feeling of Florida, especially when the sky is blue and the sun is shining.

The access is easy straight of the A9 motorway and there are 2050 parking spaces, with the first two hours being free of charge. The tram also runs to Odysseum from the city centre. Tramline 1, the blue tram with white birds, terminates at this fun-filled site, unique in this part of France.

In the commercial centre there are over a hundred shops with all the famous brand names for fashion and home you would expect to find, including Casino Geant, a very large hypermarket. The shops in the commercial centre are open from 10am to 8pm Monday to Saturday and the hypermarket is open slightly longer from 9am to 9pm, again Monday to Saturday.

Planetarium Galilee

The 156 seater theatre with its semi-circular screen allows you to be totally enveloped by the stars and planets that wrap around our Earth. There are different presentations and events including ones especially for children. For anyone keen to learn more about space travel there are reconstructions and documentaries about space travel and astronauts.

There are several exhibitions and a shop for those essential space related souvenirs. The Planetarium opens from 1.30pm onwards and is open every day in the school holidays. Other weeks it is open at weekends and Wednesdays. The admission price is €7 for adults and €6 for children to the Planetarium. There are many special events on and the times and prices do vary.

Aquarium Mare Nostrum

One of the tanks in here measures an impressive 18 metres by 9.5 metres and it is one of the largest in Europe. There is a lot more than just 400 species of fish to see as there are simulated hurricanes and South Sea storms to experience

The aquarium is open every day for all of July and August from 10am to 10pm. The rest of the year the opening times are Sunday to Thursday 10am to 7pm and Friday and Saturday 10am to 8pm. Expect to pay €15,50 for adults, children's tickets vary between €7.50 and €12.50 but there are various ticket combinations available.

Karting & Bowling

The 40 lane bowling alley is great fun and for small children there are 6 specially designed lanes. There is also a soft play area, a billiards room and an indoor karting track with a bar and snack bar for recharging your batteries. The opening hours are from noon everyday until 1am Sunday to Thursday, 2am Friday and 3am Saturday. The price for the Karting is €15 and the bowling varies between €4 and €7.

Ice Skating

There is plenty of room to skate and not just on flat ice while the DJ plays the top sounds to keep things moving. The ice rink is unusual as it has a special area with a slope as well as a tunnel to skate through lit with multi-coloured bulbs.

In school holidays the ice rink is open every night and some mornings. The rest of the year it is closed Tuesday mornings but open morning and afternoon and then three nights a week. The ice rink does close for a lunch break. Skate hire is around €3 and the admission price is €5 for adults and €4 for under 16's.

Odysseum Activities

If all the above isn't enough there is a climbing wall to test stamina and strength and a mini-park for young children. For a special meal out take the children to the Pirates Paradise, a themed restaurant or listen to some live music at the Irish pub most nights. There are 16 restaurants to choose from so there is bound to be something to suit everyone.

Fabre Museum

39 Boulevard Bonne Nouvelle
Montpellier
Tel: +33 4671 48300
www.museefabre.montpellier-agglo.com/

In 1802 a donation to the city of 30 paintings became the basis of a small museum in the town housed in a hotel. Several years later in 1825 François-Xavier Fabre generously added a large amount of his works to the collection and the Hôtel Massillian was duly refurbished and was renamed as the Fabre Museum.

Other artists soon followed Fabre's example and by 1877 nearly one thousand items had been donated by Alfred Bruvas, Jules Canonge and Jules Bonnet-Mel from their own private collections.

From 2003 to 2007 the museum had a 21st century makeover costing 61.2 million and is now classified by the French Ministry of Culture as a Museum of France. The museum building is just a short stroll along a tree-lined avenue from the Place de la Comédie and Gare St. Roch and is easy to find.

The museum is open every day except Mondays from 10am to 6pm. Ticket prices vary widely for everyone, depending on residency, age and whether it is a guided tour or not. All the prices are on the website.

Montpellier Zoo

50 Avenue Agropolis,
Montpellier
Tel: +33 4996 14550
www. zoo.montpellier.fr/

Montpellier zoo is to the north of the city and there is a really varied selection of animals. There are zebras, giraffes, rhinos plus a mixture of South American birds and African mammals. The zoo makes for a great day out as the admission is free unless you want to visit the Amazonian greenhouse. The greenhouse is fascinating and the seven climatic zones are home to more than 500 animals including tarantulas, piranhas and snakes. To make them feel at home there is an artificial rainstorm created every two hours.

The park itself is beautiful even if you don't visit the greenhouse with plenty of walks and a 20 hectare nature reserve. Access by car and public transport easy but it is quite a long walk from the nearest tram line stop at St. Eloi but there is a connecting bus to the zoo

An adult ticket is €6.50 and children pay €3. The zoo is open from 9.30am until 6.30pm from 1st April until 30th September. The rest of the year the zoo opens at 10am and closes an hour or so earlier. All the hours are on the zoo website.

Château Flaugergues

1744 Avenue Albert Einstein
Montpellier,
Tel: +33 4995 26637
www.flaugergues.com

There are many follies in the Languedoc-Roussillon area and the Château de Flaugergues near Montpellier is just one of them. The wealthy merchants and aristocrats who built the castles were servants to the French king and they filled their beautiful homes with priceless furniture and tapestries.

Etienne de Flaugergues bought his land in 1696 and starting building but it took him 45 years to complete the château. In 1811 the estate was purchased by the Boussairolles family and it was this family that designed the gardens and orangery. The gardens cover nearly four hectares and are immaculate with neatly clipped box hedges, a vineyard and some very English- style flower gardens.

There is an on-site restaurant serving excellent cuisine in beautiful surroundings. The Folia restaurant is open from 12 noon until 2.30pm. Local produce is used and the menu is planned according to the season.

An accompanied visit of the château and gardens cost €9.50 for adults and €7 for children and concessions. There are different visits with different prices available for just the gardens only, and/or the wine cellars and a wine and cheese tasting session. Château Flaugergues gardens are open all year round, apart from Sundays and bank holidays from 9.30am to 12.30pm and 14.30 to 7pm.

In June, July and September the gardens open on Sunday and bank holidays but only in the afternoon. The interior of the château is open in June, July and September from 2.30pm to 7pm but not on Mondays. The rest of the year is by appointment only, except for on Sundays.

Royal Square of Peyrou

Montpellier
Tel: +33 4676 06060

The wide tree-lined promenade of the Royal Square of Peyrou is a favourite place for the locals to stroll and enjoy the air. The statue of Louis XIV on horseback is a focal point along with the Arch de Triomphe and the Château d'Eau. Under the 18th century aqueduct on a Saturday there is a second-hand book market and organic food stalls. The belvedere was completed in 1774 to celebrate the accession of Louis XVI to the throne and offers a panoramic view of the city.

The square is very pretty when the sun goes down and the city lights are sparkling. In the months of June and July the opening hours are 7am to midnight. The rest of the year the park opens at 7am but closes at 9.30pm, and slightly earlier in November, December and January at 8pm. Admission is free.

St. Peter's Cathedral

6 Rue l'Abbé Marcel Montels
Montpellier
Tel: +33 4676 60412
www.catholique-montpellier.cef.fr/

Montpellier Cathedral is the seat of the archbishops of Montpellier as well as being a national monument of France. The cathedral started life as a humble church attached to the Saint Benoît monastery founded in 1364. The church was elevated to cathedral status in 1536 due to the see of Maquelonne being transferred to Montpellier on the orders of King François I.

The approach to the front of the cathedral is striking. The front of the 14th century building has two rocket-shaped pillars each measuring 4.55 metres in diameter. These pillars support an impressive arched canopy of stone which leads into the cathedral.

The war between the Catholics and Protestants in the 16th century meant the cathedral suffered severe damage but it was rebuilt again the following century. The interior reveals a magnificent organ case and a stunning vaulted nave. In the right-hand transept the 17th century altarpiece is a delight for the eyes and well worth a visit.

One of the well-known Protestant painters of the 17th century was Sébastien Bourdon who was born in Montpellier. He spent much of his life in Paris but from 1657 to 1658 he returned to Montpellier to paint The Fall of Simon the Magician. The painting was hung over the main altar in the cathedral and is still there today.

The cathedral is open Monday to Saturday 9am to 7pm and Sunday 9am to 1pm, Admission is free.

Château de La Mosson

Route De Lodève
Montpellier
Tel: +33 4676 06060

Joesph Bonnier was a rich banker in Montpellier and to display his wealth he purchased the Mosson estate in 1710 and work on the château started in 1723. The building was completed by 1729 and the Mosson family lived in the sumptuous château with its lavishly decorated gardens for many years. The Bonnier wealth didn't last and the family went bankrupt leaving the château to be used as factories and workshops for silks, soaps and dyes.

The city of Montpellier acquired the estate in 1982 and for many years has been trying to restore the building and gardens to their former glory. The 15 hectare park of the estate is well worth exploring along with the remains of the building itself as there is a lot of history in the area. The gardens are a public park now with free admission. The only reminder now of Bonnier's folly is the Baroque fountain and some of the statues.

Museum of Anatomy & the Faculty of Medicine

3 Rue Delmas
Montpellier
Tel: +33 4670 24769

A visit to Montpellier would not be complete without taking time to see the amazing, and sometimes gruesome, collections in the Museum of Anatomy. It is the largest anatomy museum in France and the exhibits rival the similar museum La Specola in Florence.

Montpellier has a long history associated with medicine and along with Strasbourg and Paris was one of the first cities in 1340 authorised to dissect corpses. By 1795 the new School of Medicine had opened in the city and in 1798 it was decided that to pass their exams all the doctors had to present an anatomical work. This rule remained in force until 1940. Meanwhile a very large collection of pieces were building up in the dean's office and in 1851 a new building was built to display this impressive collection.

Visitors today with nerves of steel and a strong stomach can go into the 15 metre high and 60 metre long gallery to see the rotten and diseased organs along with mummies and sections of the brain. Formalin has long been the preservative of choice for specimens in years gone by and there are plenty to see here. Deformed foetuses float eerily round in their glass wombs while skulls grin down at their audience while seeing nothing from sightless eye sockets.

Despite the marvels of modern technology that can take photographs and scans of inside the human body there is still a certain educational value in seeing the actual parts.

There are nearly 6,000 items in the collection and a two hour tour is organised by the Montpellier Tourist Office in Place de la Comédie to see this exceptional site of medical history. All the information is on the tourist office website; www.ot-montpellier.fr/en/

Montpellier Historical Centre

Between the Place de la Comédie and the Peyrou Arch are the old quarters of Montpellier. Due to its original shape the Place de la Comédie is known to the locals as l'OEuf (the Egg) and the ovoid shape comes from being built on the ramparts that surrounded the ancient city. The pedestrianised square with its central statue of the Three Graces is one of the largest city squares in Europe.

The narrow, winding streets of the city centre hide many little shops, cafés and restaurants and you can enjoy the simple pleasure of walking and listening to birdsong rather than the hum of traffic. There are numerous places to get a cup of decent French coffee accompanied by a delicious pastry of two, or maybe a glass of wine and some snails or frogs legs.

Many of the buildings in the city centre date back to medieval times but some were improved between the 16th and 18th centuries. Take time and admire the architecture of the beautiful private homes, some of the façades are remarkable and wrought iron gates lead through to hidden courtyards and staircases.

Henri Prades Museum

390, route de Pérols
34970 Lattes
Montpellier
Tel: +33 4679 97720
www.museearcheo.montpellier-agglo.com/

It was only by luck that the ancient city of Lattara was found after a field was deep-ploughed in 1963. Henri Prades along with the Painlevé Archaeological Group (GAP) decided that the site showed great promise for studying Gallic civilization as it moved forward into the Roman Era.

This ancient port was active for over 800 years and many populations used Lattara as the cultural and economic centre of the western Mediterranean. Celtic populations as well as Etruscans, Romans, Greeks and Iberians all passed through as they traded their goods with other cultures.

On the edge of the site in the old Saint-Sauveur farmhouse there is more than just a museum; there is an archaeological centre, research laboratories, a library and the excavation headquarters. The museum holds the fascination collections from the archaeological digs that have taken place over the years.

To visit the museum is free on the first Sunday of every month, on other days the admission fee is €2,50. The opening hours are Monday, Wednesday, Thursday, Friday from 10am to 12 noon and 1.30pm to 5.30pm.Saturday and Sunday 2pm to 6pm. Closed on Tuesday.

Antigone District

The Antigone District lies to the east of the historical centre of Montpellier and the 36 hectare site was developed in the late 1970's to expand the city out towards the River Lez. The project became the subject of much public interest worldwide and was one of the biggest developments in France ever to be completed.

The Catalan architect Ricardo Bofill was the man given the mammoth task of designing the development. He had to include everything a new city would need from local shops and public facilities to government buildings and offices. Much of the housing is low cost and is situated in a network of plazas and tree-lined boulevards. The Esplanade de l'Europe is a very impressive curved apartment building facing the open space of the Plaza de Thessalie.

The Antigone District is worth a visit just to admire the neo-classical architecture. There are many columns, pilasters, pediments and entablatures on a gigantic scale which gives the whole area a monumental aspect.

Botanical Gardens

Boulevard Henri IV
Montpellier
Tel: +33 4676 34322
www.univ-montp1.fr

The Botanical Gardens in Montpellier were established in 1593 and are France's oldest botanical gardens. When a similar garden was created in Paris in 1626 it was modelled on the Montpellier garden.

The 4.5 hectare garden contains 500 native Mediterranean plants and about 2,100 non-native. Roughly two thirds of the plants are grown outside and the rest under glass. The garden is divided into sections making it easier to browse through your favourite plant and in the systematic garden the plants are classified by the Bentham and Hooker system.

Other sections include medical plants, palm trees, arboretum, succulents, the cold greenhouse and orangery and finally a warm greenhouse with tropical and aquatic plants.

The Botanical Gardens are looked after by the Montpellier University and open every afternoon except Monday. The garden is classified as a Historical Monument and Protected Site and admission is free.

Château de la Mogère

2235 Route de Vauguiéres
Montpellier
Tel: +33 4676 57201
www.lamogere.fr/

The Renaissance style Château de la Mogére was designed by architect Jean Giral for a Secretary of State called Fulcran Limouzin. Giral's original design is still closely adhered to and the appearance of the château has hardly changed over the centuries. Viewed from the far end of the garden the symmetry of the château is apparent against the green of the pine forest. The wide sweeping steps lead up to the house with 18 pairs of matching white shutters keeping the French sunshine out.

The château and the gardens are open to the public and there are plenty of antique paintings and family portraits to see. Jacques-Louis David, Jean Jouvenet and Hyacinthe Rigaud are just three of the artists that have contributed their work to this wonderful collection. There are many fine examples of Louis XIV and XV in the château all beautifully preserved. The gardens are very pretty especially the fountain. A number of cherubs decorate the water feature which is made out of thousands of seashells.

Access is easy to Château La Mogére as it is right next to the auto route A9 and is opposite the Odysseum. The Montpellier tramway line stops at the Oysseum which is a ten minute walk to the château.

Admission prices for the gardens and château are €6 for adults and €3 for children. For access to the gardens only it is €3 each. The opening hours are 1st June to 30th September from 2.30pm to 6.30pm every day. From 1st January to 31st May and 1st October to 31st December Château La Mogére is open Saturdays, Sundays and national holidays. Other days can be arranged by appointment.

Esplanade Charles de Gaulle

Part of any holiday in this well-known wine growing region should include some tastings. From July through to September there is a wine festival every Friday evening from 6.30pm to 11.30pm in the Esplanade de Charles de Gaulle. For €5 you get a wine glass to keep and three tasting tickets. Wander round the 35 stalls and soak up the ambience while deciding which wine to sample. There are food stalls as well and many people buy a few snacks then sit and relax on the grass listening to the live band.

Recommendations for the Budget Traveller

Places To Stay

Montpellier Hostel

Rue des Ecoles Laiques
Impasse Petite Corraterie
Montpellier
Tel: +33 4676 03222

The Montpellier is a 94 bed hostel right in the heart of the city, close to all the shops, bars and major attractions. The room price includes breakfast and the hostel offers free Wifi, pool table, football table and has its own bar. There is a storage room at the hostel for luggage and cycle hire is available close by.

Different size dorms are available, both single sex and mixed. Prices are from around €20 per person per night.

Les Arbousiers

1022 Rue de Las Sorbes
Montpellier
Tel: +33 6151 06739
www.dauzac.org/

Les Arbousiers is a family run guest house that is close to all the attractions that Montpellier has to offer. There are five bedrooms, some with access to the large balcony. There are no ensuite rooms but ample bathrooms and showers for sharing.

The house is set in a pleasant garden full of flowers and trees and is ideal for a peaceful stay but still handy for the centre. There is free car parking outside on the street and the tram stop is close by for a quick trip into the city centre.

Expect to pay from €30 per person per night which includes breakfast with the family. Dinner with the family can be booked in advance and it is a good way to practice your French. Don't worry if you are not fluent as the father speaks very good English.

La Farigoule

13 av du General Grollier
Pignan
Montpellier
Tel: +33 4672 70894
www.lafarigoule34.com/

A few kilometres away from Montpellier is the La Farigoule guest house. The house is in the typical Languedoc style and was originally a wine-growers house. There are only three rooms, all with one double bed and one single bed. The rooms have en-suite facilities and are all beautifully decorated.

Prices per night for three people sharing a room are €80 per room, two sharing €62 per room and for one person €52 per room. A light continental breakfast is included. There is a very pretty terrace with honey coloured stone walls and tumbling flowers where breakfast is served when the weather permits. In the colder months there is a pleasant dining room with a large fireplace.

La Vagance

155 rue des Escarceliers
Montpellier
Tel: +33 4674 02935
www.lavagance.fr/

La Vagance is set in a tranquil suburb of Montpellier in lush gardens with lots of palm trees framing the south facing breakfast terrace. There are two rooms, the Iris Room with a double bed and the Grand Cèdre with twin beds. Both rooms are spacious with comfortable beds and en-suite showers. Breakfast is included and rates are from €37.50 per person per night for two people sharing. There are special rates for three night breaks and longer stays.

Sweet Home 34

15 rue Claude Chappe
Montpellier
Tél : +33 4995 19932
www.sweet-home34.fr/

Sweet Home 34 guest house is only a short distance from the historic centre of Montpellier and all the beautiful architecture that the city offers. Closer to this relaxing guest house are the clean and modern lines of the Antigone District with its shops, bars and restaurants to enjoy.

There are five rooms in Sweet Home 34 to choose from, some with king size beds, some with doubles. Some of the rooms have private facilities but not all of them. All the rooms have air conditioning and Wifi. The prices are from €55 per person per night for two people sharing a room and this includes breakfast.

Places To Eat & Drink

Playfood

16, Boulevard Louis Blanc
Montpellier
Tel: +33 4342 26152
www.playfood.fr

For a different dining experience find Playfood on the gentle curving Boulevard Louis Blanc, it isn't hard to find as one of the tram lines runs right down the centre of the street. The restaurant inside has a modern feel and there are wooden chairs and tables outside for dining al fresco.

Playfood serves food in verrines. Verrines are small thick glasses that contain food rather than liquids. There is a wide variety of hot or cold, sweet or savoury treats to choose from including a good vegetarian selection. All the verrines are sold individually and cost around €2-€2.50 each. Playfood is open from Tuesday to Saturday from 7.30pm to midnight.

Le P'tit Mas

30, avenue Pierre d'Adhemar
Montpellier
Tel: +33 4675 72581

The snack bar and café is popular with locals for its cosy and friendly atmosphere and good food. Some of the house specialties are grilled prawns and cuttlefish, oysters and a selection of delicious sounding salads. Le P'tit Mas is open from 8am to 10.30pm all week except for Saturday evenings.

The café is family friendly and groups are welcome. A decent meal and drinks is around €15 while the menu of the day is €11. There is a large terrace outside with a nice view where you can sit and watch the word pass by.

Le Pescator

23 pl. du Nombre d'Or
Montpellier
Tel: +33 4671 32916
www.restaurant-lepescator-montpellier.fr

The brightly coloured bar complete with portholes when you enter Le Pescator sets the nautical theme for your meal of freshly caught fish and shellfish. With jazz music playing gently in the background you can ponder over the á la carte or daily menus.

The three course menu costs €30 and has enticing dishes like Monkfish Provençal, Smoked Red Scottish Salmon and Bream or for non-fish eaters there is a Fillet of Beef. If you are in hurry just have a quick meal of Mussels and Chips for €14.

Le Pescator is open every day for lunch and dinner, the restaurant has air-conditioning and there is a shady terrace for eating out on summer days.

Pain et Cie

4 Place Jean Jaurès
Montpellier
Tel: +33 4676 02435
www.painetcompagnie.fr/

Pain et Cie is a great place to eat right in the heart of the city and to meet people. In the centre of the restaurant is a large communal table where you can join in and get to know locals and visitors alike. There are three smaller rooms with seating for a more intimate experience as well as a large shaded terrace. The restaurant serves good home cooked food in huge portions all with a regional flavour. Try the breaded and fried cheese wheel as a starter and you might not want a main course.

The waitresses are fast and efficient and do speak a little English. Pain et Cie is open all day seven days a week for breakfast, lunch and dinner. They also sell a range of breads, jams and spices to takeaway.

Times Café

7-9 Rue des Teissiers
Montpellier
Tel: +33 4675 49842

The Times Café celebrated its tenth anniversary in 2011 and is considered to be one of the best wine bars in the city. It is a super place to meet friends and enjoy a selection of French wines accompanied by a selection of bite-sized snacks.

Tasty French bread with olives, sun-dried tomatoes plus foie gras and fig jam are just some of the items on the menu. There is a wide selection of platters to sample with fish, meat and vegetarian options. Opening hours are Monday to Saturday from 6.30pm to 1am.

Places To Shop

Les Halles Castellane

Place Castellane
Montpellier

To get a feel for how the French do their shopping have a wander round Les Halles Castellane. Lose yourself in the hustle and bustle of the daily market and enjoy all the tempting aromas of fresh bread mingling with espresso coffee as well as the butchers, fishmongers and fruit and vegetable stalls.

Stock up on some cold meats and cheese, pop in a bottle of wine and some crusty bread and go for a picnic. Montpellier has some beautiful open spaces to lunch in the fresh air. For an alternative there are pizza stalls and octopus pies from the little city of Sète close by. The market is open Monday to Saturday from 7.30am to 7.30pm, Sundays and bank holidays from 7.30am to 3pm.

Peyrou Plaza

Jardins du Peyrou
Montpellier
Tel: +33 6227 70721

This is a great place for bargain hunters and the perfect place to spend a Sunday morning. The antique dealers and secondhand stalls can hide all sorts of undiscovered treasures. There are decorative items for the home, used and old books plus fancy and unusual goods are all there waiting to be found.

There is usually live music playing and there are places to eat, drink and soak up the atmosphere. Be there early to get the best bargains, the market opens at 7.30am to 2pm and there is free car parking in the Arceaux nearby.

Images du Demain

10, rue de la Vieille
Montpellier
Tel: +33 4676 62345
www.carterie-encadrement-montpellier.com/

Many visitors like to take a painting or print home as a reminder of their holiday. This is the shop to find just that souvenir and the choice is vast. Be prepared to spend a while searching the walls of the alley outside the shop for the right picture.

There are maps, prints, postcards, drawings and posters in all sizes and with prices to suit all budgets. The friendly and helpful staff will do their best to find the best picture to suit your taste. Images du Demain is open Monday to Saturday from 9.30am to 7.30pm.

Le Boutik'R

41 Boulevard Bonne Nouvelle
Montpellier
Tel: +33 4676 63593
www.leboutikr.fr/

A visit to Le Boutik'R must be part of any holiday in Montpellier. The city as well as the Languedoc Roussillon region has many talented arts and crafts workers and examples of their work can be found here. The shop opened in 2008 in a beautiful old mansion with high, vaulted ceilings and offers a range of home ware and linen as well as a variety of home produced food and wine.

The owners are passionate about quality and authenticity and the shop has the Quality Hérault label as many of the items stocked are local to the area. Le Boutik'R is open 10am to 7pm Tuesday to Saturday and 1pm to 6pm on Sunday. The shop is very close to the Fabré Museum and Place du Comédie.

Etat d'Ame

12 Rue en Gondeau
Montpellier
Tel: +33 4676 07920

An explosion of colour awaits you as soon as you enter Etat d'Ame. The shop sells china, brightly coloured linens, and novelty items like flattened bottle-tops made into chandeliers. The long table that greets you is full of Polish handmade cups, bowls and plates; none of which match but that is part of the charm.

To add to this rainbow tea party there are vintage toys and old cinema chairs imported from India. To browse among these items Etat d'Ame is open Monday to Saturday 9am to 6pm.

Made in the USA
Columbia, SC
31 March 2023

14595309R00043